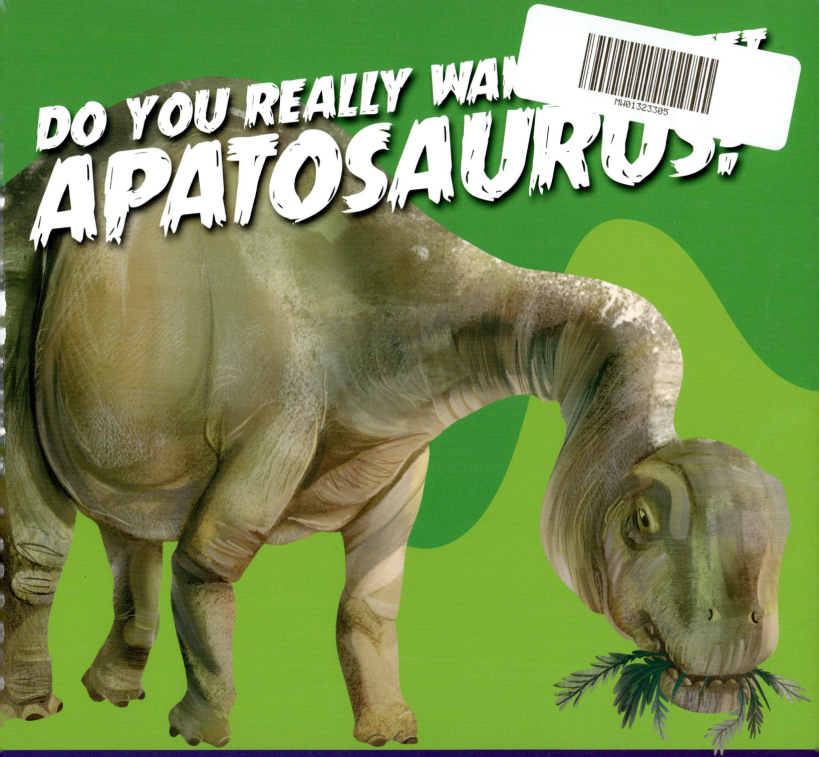

DO YOU REALLY WANT AN APATOSAURUS?

BY ANNETTE BAY PIMENTEL • ILLUSTRATED BY DANIELE FABBRI

AMICUS ILLUSTRATED and **AMICUS INK**
are published by Amicus
P.O. Box 1329, Mankato, MN 56002
www.amicuspublishing.us

COPYRIGHT © 2018 AMICUS. International copyright reserved in all countries. No part of this book may be reproduced in any form without written permission from the publisher.

EDITOR: Rebecca Glaser
DESIGNER: Kathleen Petelinsek

LIBRARY OF CONGRESS CATALOGING-IN-PUBLICATION DATA
Names: Pimentel, Annette Bay, author. | Fabbri, Daniele, 1978- illustrator.
Title: Do you really want to meet Apatosaurus? / by Annette Bay Pimentel ; illustrated by Daniele Fabbri.
Other titles: Do you really want to meet...?
Description: Mankato, Minnesota : Amicus Illustrated, [2018] | Series: Do you really want to meet a dinosaur? | Audience: K to grade 3.
Identifiers: LCCN 2016057202 (print) | LCCN 2016058704 (ebook) | ISBN 9781681511122 (library binding) | ISBN 9781681521374 (pbk.) | ISBN 9781681512020 (ebook)
Subjects: LCSH: Apatosaurus—Juvenile literature. | CYAC: Dinosaurs.
Classification: LCC QE862.S3 P5575 2018 (print) | LCC QE862.S3 (ebook) | DDC 567.913/8—dc23
LC record available at https://lccn.loc.gov/2016057202

Printed in China
HC 10 9 8 7 6 5 4 3 2 1
PB 10 9 8 7 6 5 4 3 2 1

ABOUT THE AUTHOR
Annette Bay Pimentel lives in Moscow, Idaho with her family. She doesn't have a time machine, so she researches the past at the library. She writes about what happened a long time ago in nonfiction picture books like *Mountain Chef* (2016, Charlesbridge). You can visit her online at www.annettebaypimentel.com.

ABOUT THE ILLUSTRATOR
Daniele Fabbri was born in Ravenna, Italy, in 1978. He graduated from Istituto Europeo di Design in Milan, Italy, and started his career as a cartoon animator, storyboarder, and background designer for animated series. He has worked as a freelance illustrator since 2003, collaborating with advertising agencies and international publishers, including many books for Amicus.

That Apatosaurus skeleton is huge! Were they huge as babies, too? You would love to see that. Do you want to meet an Apatosaurus and find out?

Of course, Apatosaurus is extinct, so you'll need a time machine! Go back 150 million years to the Jurassic Period. Scientists have found Apatosaurus fossils in Colorado, so head there. Leave your winter coat behind. It was warm all year back then.

In the Jurassic Period, Colorado was mostly flat. The grassy plains were similar to an African savanna today.

That puddle is nearly the size of a toddler's wading pool. But don't dive in! It's an Apatosaurus footprint. Follow the tracks to the giant dinosaur!

There's the foot that made the footprint. Better not stand close. Apatosaurus is enormous! It stretches as long as two school buses and weighs more than three elephants. One stomp would crush you flat.

But don't worry about getting eaten. Apatosaurus only eats plants. It doesn't move its big body much to find food. It just swings its long neck around to graze on plants growing near the ground. It swallows without chewing.

A dinosaur stomps by. It's a meat-eater, Allosaurus. It eats young and sick Apatosauruses. But this full-grown, healthy Apatosaurus doesn't even flinch. It's too big for Allosaurus to take on.

You're a lot smaller, though. Better move on.

Don't trip over those bumps! Those are buried dinosaur eggs. Each one is a bit smaller than a soccer ball. There's a cracked shell.

And here are tiny tracks! Each track is only about 3 inches (7.6 cm) long. Follow the tracks to the baby dinosaurs!

It's a whole herd of baby Apatosauruses! They're so cute—and little! Each one is only about the size of a puppy now. They'll grow fast.

Watch out! There's a big snake! Snakes hunt baby dinosaurs. These Apatosauruses are in danger.

Oh no! The snake got one of the babies! The others are running away on their two back legs. Grown-up Apatosauruses can't do that. But it helps little ones move faster.

They'll get away. Time to go back to your own time. Now you've seen them with your own eyes. One of the world's largest dinosaurs was once small, too.

WHERE HAVE APATOSAURUS FOSSILS BEEN FOUND?

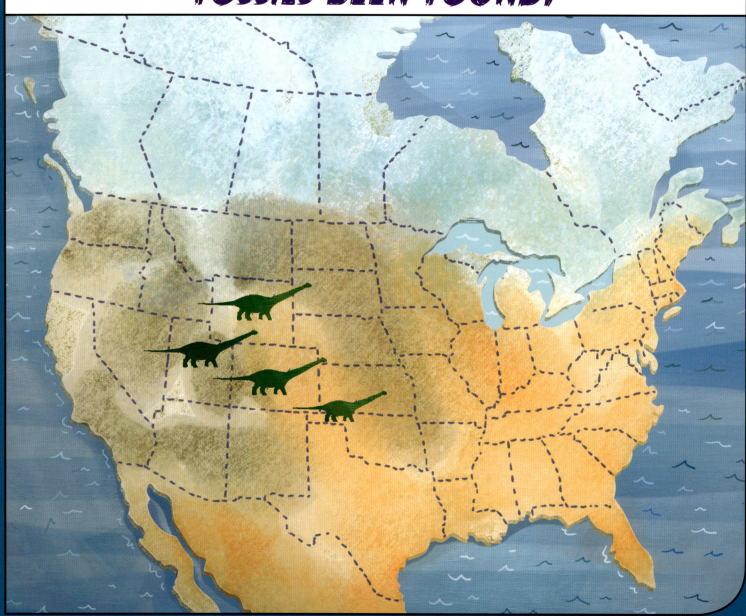

GLOSSARY

extinct—No longer found living anywhere in the world.

fossil—A bone or other trace of an animal from millions of years ago, preserved as rock.

herd—A group of animals that live together.

Jurassic Period—Time period from 200 million to 145 million years ago.

savanna—A flat, grassy plain with few or no trees.

AUTHOR'S NOTE

Too bad for us, time machines aren't real. But all of the details about Apatosaurus in this book are based on research by scientists who study fossils. For example, in 2010 scientists announced they had discovered footprints left by baby Apatosauruses. The tracks were made only by the dinosaurs' back feet, suggesting it could run on two legs! New dinosaur discoveries are made every year. Look up the books and websites below to learn more.

READ MORE

Alpert, Barbara. *Apatosaurus.* Mankato, Minn.: Amicus, 2014.

Gray, Susan H. *Apatosaurus (Exploring Dinosaurs).* Mankato, Minn.: Child's World, 2015.

Lee, Sally. *Apatosaurus (Little Paleontologist).* North Mankato, Minn.: Capstone Press, 2015.

WEBSITES

APATOSAURUS: DK FIND OUT
http://www.dkfindout.com/us/dinosaurs-and-prehistoric-life/dinosaurs/apatosaurus/
Learn more about the Apatosaurus and its eggs.

DINOSAURS: NATIONAL GEOGRAPHIC KIDS
http://kids.nationalgeographic.com/explore/nature/dinosaurs/
Compare sizes of dinosaurs, meet paleontologists, and more.

Every effort has been made to ensure that these websites are appropriate for children. However, because of the nature of the Internet, it is impossible to guarantee that these sites will remain active indefinitely or that their contents will not be altered.